Martin Edmond

Ghost Who Writes

FOUR
WINDS
PRESS

MONTANA
Estates
Essay Series

Cover artwork: **Jacqui Colley**
Author photograph: **Bruce Foster**

Martin Edmond was born
in Ohakune, 1952; raised in
Greytown, Huntly, Upper Hutt,
Auckland ... then away.
One of the Aotearoan disapora
now returned "home" for an
indeterminate period of time.
Has authored five books and
five films.

www.fourwindspress.co.nz

Ghost Who Writes

MONTANA
Estates

Essay Series

Other titles by Martin Edmond

CHRONICLE OF THE UNSUNG

FENUA IMI: THE PACIFIC IN HISTORY AND IMAGINARY

THE RESURRECTION OF PHILIP CLAIRMONT

CHEMICAL EVOLUTION:

DRUGS AND ART PRODUCTION 1970-80

THE AUTOBIOGRAPHY OF MY FATHER

Ghost Who Writes

Martin Edmond

Series editor: Lloyd Jones

FOUR
WINDS
PRESS

Four Winds Press
Wellington

ISBN 0-9582514-3-6

First published September 2004

Airplane Studios
Typeset in Perpetua

Printed by Printlink

... it is not private thinking but, as Brecht once expressed it, the art of thinking in other people's heads that is decisive.

— Walter Benjamin

1

In 1935, the Portuguese poet Fernando Pessoa believed he had two more years to live: time enough at last to order his literary papers. His horoscope, which he cast himself, made this certain. Unfortunately, as his literary friend and fellow occultist Raul Leal realised, Pessoa had made a mistake in the casting; but he hadn't the heart to tell him. Pessoa died on 30 November 1935, in Lisbon, leaving behind a trunk containing 27,543 documents organised in a way only he understood.

Those documents were written by one man, but that man wrote under 72 different names: like the 72 letters of the name of god. His own name, *Pessoa*, means *person*, or *persona*; it is old – there was a Pero Pessoa employed as a factor in Portuguese

Malacca in 1512. Perhaps it was the anonymity of Pessoa which generated the drive towards other identities.

He called those multitudes under whose names he wrote *heteronyms*, adapting to literary usage a term hitherto employed to describe certain anomalous linguistic facts: the same word with different sounds and meanings, different words for the same thing. But what is the relationship of a heteronym to the author who writes him (or her: Pessoa's heteronyms include a hunchback girl called Maria José)?

It gets stranger. For those works written under his own name, Pessoa used another word, *orthonym*, meaning *real name*; by this sleight of language making it seem that even when he was writing as himself, he was still someone else. His own non-existence as a personality is a central insistence in Pessoa's work; paradoxically, from this insistence arises his ability to empathise with the existences of others. Pessoa the hermetic, the rarefied, has more passages of acute recognition of the dilemma of the common man or woman than any comparable writer (except that there are no comparable writers).

His great poem, *Tobacco Shop* by Alvaro de Campos, begins with a confession of utter nullity – *I'm nothing/I'll always be nothing/I can't even wish to be something/Apart from that, I've got all the world's dreams inside me* – and ends with a revelation of the ordinary existence of others – *... 'Hello, Stevens!' and the universe/Re-organizes itself for me, without hopes or ideals, and the Tobacco Shop Owner smiles.*

Pessoa gave his life's work the title *Fictions of the Interlude*. It was to include the writings of all his heteronyms, excluding only semi-heteronym Bernardo Soares' *Book of Disquiet*. The interlude is the time between birth and death, as if consciousness itself were only a brief flare between two darknesses, and made up entirely of inventions of various kinds.

The questions raised by Pessoa's heteronymic project are multiple and mostly unanswerable: is it a master plan never put into execution or a splendid ruin? An act of despair or a triumph? An example of total idiosyncrasy or a strategy with wider applications and implications? What can we learn about authorship from one who refused the simplicity of his own name?

In a literary essay written in English, Pessoa calls Shakespeare *the greatest failure in literature*: a startling proposition. He also suggests that Shakespeare must have been aware of this. Shakespeare's famous impersonality is interrogated in the essay, and found to have its source in both his temperament and his life experience. Pessoa divines that what he calls *unappreciation* poisoned Shakespeare's mind: he had to spend his life engaged in theatrical hackwork, when he was capable of so much more:

> Great as his tragedies are, none of them is greater
> than the tragedy of his own life. The gods gave
> him all great gifts but one; the one they gave not
> was the power to use those great gifts greatly …
> his creative power was shattered into a thousand

fragments by the stress and oppression of life.
It is but shreds of itself. Disjecta membra, said
Carlyle, are what we have of any poet, or of any
man. Of no poet or man is this truer than of
Shakespeare.

It is not hard to intuit that, writing of Shakespeare, Pessoa was also writing of himself. He once compared his heteronymic panoply to a cast of characters without a play, a sequence of soliloquists who appear, not on the stage, but on the page and therefore in the interior theatre of the mind. The question is, are any writer's works different? What is the act of writing and how does it work?

St Augustine, in the fourth century of the common era, was the first person in history to read without moving his lips. In other words, the first to read without saying the words aloud, even if that "aloud" is understood as silently aloud. Without moving his lips: the words he read went from the page, via the eyes, into his mind, their status as oral facts concealed in the transition.

Even so, whether accomplished in silence or out loud, all reading and all writing does involve the act of mentally speaking the words. This is analogous to the interior monologue most of us engage in for most of our waking moments.

And if, however occluded it may be, mental speaking is intrinsic to the act of reading, does this mean that when we read we are inhabited by the projected voice of the author we are reading, hosting him or her the way an organism hosts a parasite or a virus?

When the American writer Richard Ford read aloud from his novel *Independence Day* at the Embassy Theatre in Wellington on the night of 9 March 2004, there was a moment between the end of his prefatory remarks and the beginning of the reading proper when his body seemed to shift slightly to one side, and upwards, if such a thing can be; a shiver went through him; and his voice, when it came, was higher pitched than it had been and seemed to have a trace, though only a trace, of a

whine in it. Richard Ford had moved aside to allow
Frank Bascombe to enter.

Or should we say to let Frank Bascombe out? Here
is Pessoa again, this time speaking of one of Dickens' characters:

> Mr Pickwick belongs to the sacred figures of the
> world's history. Do not, please, claim that he has
> never existed: the same thing happens to most
> of the world's sacred figures, and they have been
> living presences to a vast number of consoled
> wretches … it is a recasting of the old pagan
> noise, the old Bacchic joy of the world being
> ours, though transiently, at the coexistence and
> fullness of men …

A vast number of consoled wretches: the readers of
this world are not usually described in this way,
but why not? Whether the consolation be philosophic, poetic, fictional, non-fictional is beside the point:
the living presence of an (insubstantial) other within
us makes our own lives a little easier to bear.

The means of this sharing is a telepathic act which is as pertinent to a software manual as to a page of Wittgenstein, to a Mills and Boon fantasy as to *The Travels of Marco Polo*.

2

Constantin Cavafy was an older contemporary of Pessoa's, born in Alexandria in 1863 and dying in the same city in 1933. Like Pessoa, he spoke English, having lived in London between the ages of nine and 16; and the two writers shared a passion for the works of Shakespeare especially, Oscar Wilde and other English writers – Robert Browning for Cavafy, Dickens for Pessoa. Like Pessoa, too, Cavafy affected English manners and dress all his life, and is said to have spoken Greek with a slight English accent.

While Pessoa spent his working life as a translator of commercial correspondence into English or

14

French for Portuguese businesses trading abroad, Cavafy was for 30 years a special clerk in the Irrigation Service (Third Circle) of the Ministry of Public Works; this income he supplemented with speculative earnings, often quite substantial, on the Egyptian Stock Exchange. (With Kafka, these two make up a triumvirate of nearly anonymous clerks who transformed European literature.)

Cavafy is remembered as a conversationalist who would on street corners in Alexandria recount salacious gossip or scandalous anecdotes, sometimes at great length, about characters who had been dead for hundreds of years. A contemporary of Pessoa's confessed that, whenever they parted after meeting in the streets of Lisbon, he never dared to look back as his friend walked away – in case he was not there.

In Pessoa's *Mensagem* (*Message*), the only book in Portuguese he published in his lifetime (there were two early books in English), both factual and legendary events in Portuguese history are incorporated into his own consciousness. Cavafy's trajectory is opposite: he sends himself into the past to become a living observer of it.

Hidden Things, a poem written in 1908 and unpublished in his lifetime, begins: *From all I did and all I said / let no-one try to find out who I was.* The poem refers to Cavafy's homosexuality which was, as an act of private disclosure, one of the major engines of his poetry. Or perhaps we should say his sexuality was just one of the forces which drove his poetry, others of which might be anonymity, historical consciousness, memory and fate.

Hidden Things ends in the conviction that *Later, in a more perfect society / someone else made just like me / is certain to appear and act freely.* That time, sooner perhaps than Cavafy thought, may already be here, though we might quibble over the phrase *more perfect*; yet a reading of Cavafy's oeuvre leaves absolutely no doubt that *later* also means *earlier*. In other words, *someone else made just like me* not only will come but has already been.

In Cavafy's world, past and present, though usually not the future, are contemporaneous. His poetry collapses the 22-odd centuries between Alexander's founding of the Hellenistic empire in the third century BC and Cavafy's own world of late nineteenth-century and early twentieth-century Alexandria. A few of his poems, like *Hidden Things*, are in his own voice, but most are not: through him speak people – usually but not always men – of other times. Some of these are historical characters; many are fictions – anonymous voices from the Seleucid Dynasty, say, or from that of the Ptolemys', or Syrians who seem, by an act of ventriloquism, to appear out of an inky blackness into the clarity of Greek light to speak their piece before disappearing again.

It is common for these anonymous or fictional characters to discuss, like Cavafy himself, the activities of real people from obscure parts of the historical record. Paradoxically, this seems to increase the reality of both fictional character and real person. Cavafy's own voice is thereby given to others as hidden as he himself wanted to be.

The eerie dimension of his reach may be illustrated with reference to *One of Their Gods*, set in Selefkia, which, founded around 312BC by Selefkos I Nicator as his imperial capital, stood on the Tigris. The poem narrates the progress of a beautiful young man through the city *toward the quarter that lives only at night*, while passers-by watch and speculate: ... *they would wonder which of Them it could be/ and for what suspicious pleasure/he'd come down into the streets of Selefkia ...*

The young man is a god come down to debauch himself among mortals. He is as veiled as the author in *Hidden Things* – and as immortal. But how can this be? It is commonplace among writers of antiquity to speak of gods coming down to earth and moving amongst men and women, but what they mean by that is as mysterious as what Cavafy means here. If we were to think of it another way, and imagine that a mortal may become for a brief period the

18

repository of the divine, possessed by some un-earthly spirit of beauty or courage or delight, then that would trouble a modern sensibility far less than what is actually said – that a god has descended and moves among us. It is something which most of us cannot in any literal sense believe.

Cavafy, characteristically, elides the difficulty by narrating the act(s) of the drama through the eyes of casual, anonymous passers-by. The effect of this is to contextualise belief in the everyday reality of the gods, to grant it to the contemporary observer while allowing the possibility that it is nothing more than a quaint superstition from times past. But the poems do not privilege a rationalist, sceptical view. Rather, they go as far as they can towards unmediated belief, without ever taking that last step into complete acceptance.

Thus, as readers, we seem to hover in suspension before a world entirely interpenetrated by the divine, or one in which history is made before our eyes; just as, in the erotic poems, we are suspended on the brink of a comprehensively eroticised reality, which is nevertheless out of reach – or reachable only in memory, whose agency is imagination: that is, the poem itself.

Not that Cavafy has no time for scepticism, which takes its place alongside belief as a vital component of the sensibility that can see the world as divine, or erotically charged, or – the third critical dimension of his work – replete with the immanence of the fates of men. It is one of the miracles of Cavafy's poetry that he can, by elaborating upon obscure addenda to history, activate so many questions yet answer none of them.

As Marguerite Yourcenar points out in her definitive introduction to the 1957 French edition of Cavafy's works, if all of his poems are entirely historical, at the same time they are all entirely personal. He is equally an inherited voice of the Hellenistic world, a conduit of memories of the past, and the site of the recurrence of remembered and re-remembered erotic encounters.

Yourcenar's account of how Cavafy constructs what she calls *a timeless self* out of contrarieties has a *claritas* which is perhaps the French equivalent of the Greek light that illuminates Cavafy's Memory Theatre. She stresses particularly the way in which he evokes this theatre through an economy of means: unadorned language, vernacular speech, a paucity of description, a resiling from lyric effusion. But his central achievement is that forging of a timeless self. For when we read Cavafy's work, from which he seems absent and yet in which he is also pervasive, his absence leaves room for us, however briefly, if not to walk that antique stage ourselves, at least to stand not far off, watching the enigmas and ambiguities of love and fate unfold. We become, in this moment of psychic legerdemain, timeless selfs ourselves.

3

The German-Jewish writer Walter Benjamin died in the small Spanish seaside border town of Portbou on 26 September 1940, apparently by his own hand. He had already spent three months in a concentration camp in France, from which he was released through the intercession of friends; he returned to Paris, but fled as the Nazi armies approached.

He had just arrived in Spain, having been guided on foot through a pass in the Pyrenees, carrying with him, despite his *angina pectoris*, a heavy briefcase containing a manuscript which, he said, was more precious than his life. Lisa Fittko, his guide, many years later wrote an extraordinary account of their journey over the mountains.

The day before they were to leave, on fairly vague instructions given by the local mayor, they walked some way into the mountains to find the path. At the point where Fittko turned back, satisfied she knew at least where the route began, *Old Benjamin*, as she called him (he was 48), announced that he would stay the night there. Nothing she could say would dissuade him from this course, so she left him there.

One of the arguments Benjamin used to justify his decision was that he had already carried his briefcase this far and it would be silly to carry it back and then out again; and he could not of course leave it behind. Next day, it turned out he had spent the night stretched out on the grass elaborating, by a process of reasoning that left his guide incredulous, exactly how many minutes – ten – he would be able to walk for before needing to rest.

Nor, as their journey proceeded, could she dissuade him from drinking water from a stinking pool, even though he risked catching typhoid: he was thirsty, he said, and it didn't matter if he got sick, so long as the manuscript arrived safely in Spain. *He couldn't act intuitively*, Fittko said. *He couldn't do anything at all until he had first developed an appropriate theory.*

At a hotel in Portbou, Benjamin was told by Spanish authorities that they now required an exit visa from France and, next day, he would be sent back to obtain one. Unable to face this prospect, it is alleged that he overdosed on morphine, a number of tablets of which he was carrying. Alleged: the circumstances around his death are complex and ambiguous, and no one has yet managed to give a clear account of exactly what happened.

The briefcase was found next to his clothed body in the hotel room. It contained his personal effects, some of which, clearly, had been removed from his pockets: his watch, his tobacco and pipe, six passport photos, an x-ray, his glasses, letters, magazines, documents and money, but no manuscript. It had disappeared, and has not been found since. Nor has anyone yet offered a convincing theory as to what this work was: suggestions include a late revision (or duplicate) of *Das Passagen-Werk*, his magnum opus on nineteenth-century Paris; an expanded version of the *Theses on the Philosophy of*

History; even some kind of politically compromising work which included a list of communist collaborators and/or traitors.

In fact, a manuscript of *Das Passagen-Werk*, along with Benjamin's sonnets and other notes, was safe in the Bibliothèque Nationale in Paris, secreted there by Benjamin's friend Georges Bataille. It is a discourse on the shopping arcades of Paris, *the capital of the nineteenth century*, and a meditation on the crowd in recent history.

Das Passagen-Werk, as the title suggests, is itself a vast labyrinth, more than 1,000 pages long, about five-sixths of which consists of quotations Benjamin derived from other sources. The remaining one-sixth, written in his own voice, consists mostly of short pieces of dense, fiercely allusive prose.

Benjamin once remarked that, if his German prose was superior to that of his contemporaries', it was because he had long since sworn off the use of the first-person singular, the authorial "I", as the voice

of his thought. He would write in the third person,
or let others speak for him. He also conceived the
ambition, never fulfilled, of composing a major
work consisting entirely of quotations. In this it
would imitate a city, where the most disparate
facts – a wig-maker; a massage parlour; a video
shop – abut against each other to make a kind of
occult order which can be deciphered only so far as
to elucidate its enigmatic splendour.

The literary figure at the heart of Benjamin's
labyrinth, the writer who spoke most eloquently
for him, is Charles Baudelaire. *Les Fleurs du mal*,
said Benjamin, was the last lyric work which had *a
European repercussion; no later work penetrated beyond a
more or less limited linguistic area.* After Baudelaire, we
are all swallowed up in the crowd.

In the same piece (*Some Motifs in Baudelaire*, XII),
Benjamin quotes from a passage of satirical prose
which, he says, has been unfairly ignored by
Baudelaire's editors. A poet, discovered in *a place of
ill repute*, is asked how he came to be there. While

hurrying to cross a boulevard, the poet replies, *midst this moving chaos in which death comes galloping at you from all sides at once*, he slipped, fell and dislodged his halo, which rolled away into the gutter. The poet did not have the courage to pick it up again and anyway decided *it hurts less to lose one's insignia than to have one's bones broken.* Besides, *Now I can go about incognito, do bad things, and indulge in vulgar behaviour like ordinary mortals.* Nor will he report his loss to the police, or inquire after the halo at the lost property office. It amuses him to think that a bad poet might pick it up and wear it, thinking it has some value or significance.

For Benjamin, this tale tells *the price for which the sensation of the modern age may be had: the disintegration of the aura in the experience of shock.* The anonymity of the self in the crowd is our true condition, one that we share with everyone, even those who pretend to be exceptional.

In Baudelaire's own *On Wine and Hashish* (1851), subtitled *Compared as a means of multiplying indi-*

viduality, and in *The Poem of Hashish* in *Les Paradis artificiels* (1860), he speaks at length of his agony at the proliferation of selves he feels during hashish intoxication, an experience which may be contrasted with Pessoa's lifelong anguish of self-less-ness. What is exemplary in both writers is their insistence on making this depersonalisation and/or proliferation of self central to their work.

Some 18 months before Benjamin's death, the Spanish poet Antonio Machado crossed the same frontier in the other direction. He was fleeing Franco's Nationalist troops at the end of the Spanish Civil War, travelling in an old car with his aged mother sitting in his lap. Within a month both had died, worn out, in the French town of Colliure, Machado predeceasing his mother by a few days.

Machado had also been carrying a briefcase full of manuscripts, but by some misadventure it was left behind in Spain, and when it turned up again it was, like Benjamin's, empty. However, in this instance, we know more or less what was in it: a number of poems by an imaginary poet called Pedro de Zuniga, a putative member of the Spanish Generation of 1927; and an anthology of imaginary future poets.

It is unclear if Machado was aware of Pessoa's heteronymic obsession, although he may well have been; perhaps it does not matter. Like Pessoa, he invented other writers apart from those lost from his briefcase, though not as many as his Portuguese contemporary. Among them are two main figures: Abel Martín, a poet-philosopher; and a student of Martín's called Juan de Mairena who, in the early 1930s, wrote a series of newspaper articles defending the Spanish Republic.

Siesta — In Memory of Abel Martín by Juan de Mairena concludes: *With our cup of darkness filled to the brim / with our heart that always knows some hunger / let us give honour to the Lord who created Zero / and carved our thought out of the block of faith.* The poem is de Mairena's elegy for his master and comes with a commentary on the philosophical implications of this and other of Martín's poems: *In the theology*

29

of Abel Martín, God is defined as absolute Being, and therefore nothing which exists could be his work. This definition harks back to the pre-Socratics, especially Empedocles, whose sphere in which all elements mingle together under the power of love is analogous to Martín's Zero.

In other words, we come from nothing and in that genesis is both our ability to conceptualise – thought begins out of the idea of zero – and, importantly, our ability to forget: ... *and since the miracle of not-being is finished/start then poet, a song at the edge of it all/to death, to silence, and to what does not return.*

There is something inexpressibly melancholy about the loss of Pedro de Zuniga and Machado's other future poets, gone back in *to the great circle of nothing* from which they came, even though that is the condition of all work, and all people. They are like war dead, whose potential for love and valour has gone under in the cataclysm; theirs are voices we have never heard and, Cavafy notwithstanding, may never hear.

It is as painful to contemplate Benjamin's lost manuscript, if indeed it was not a version of something which has survived in another form; almost all his late work is anyway fragmentary. But if he was a man who could not act intuitively, that does not mean he could not write prophetically. In his last surviving work, the *Theses on the Philosophy of History*, he wrote (about a Paul Klee work in his possession):

> This is how one pictures the angel of history. Its face is turned towards the past. Where we perceive a chain of events, he sees one single catastrophe which keeps piling wreckage on wreckage and hurls it in front of his feet. The angel would like to stay, awaken the dead, make whole what has been smashed. But a storm is blowing from Paradise; it has got caught in his wings with such violence the angel can no longer close them. This storm irresistibly propels him into the future to which his back is turned, while the pile of debris before him grows skyward. This storm is what we call progress.

German writer W. G. Sebald's first publication
in English was *The Emigrants* (1996), which had
previously appeared in Germany, in 1993, as *Die
Ausgewanerten*; like all of the books which were
published during his lifetime, its translation into
English was overseen by the author, in such a
manner that it is difficult to believe that the original
was written in another language. Like Cavafy's
and Pessoa's, then, Sebald's work has an organic
connection to English literature.

Sebald sometimes used the word "novel" – *Roman*,
in German – to describe the four books he wrote
and published in the last decade of his life: in English, and in the order of their German composition,
Vertigo; The Emigrants; The Rings of Saturn; Austerlitz.
At other times he spoke of *prose works of indeterminate form.*

The Emigrants begins with the unnamed narrator
and his companion, Clara, driving out to a place

called Hingham in East Anglia *in search of somewhere to live*. In that same first sentence we learn that the narrator is about to take up a position in Norwich, where the real W.G. Sebald taught for over 30 years. What follows in the next 20-odd pages is a seemingly straightforward description of the place they go to see, a brief account of the almost entirely uneventful period they spend living there, followed by a summary of further contacts they had with a certain Dr Henry Selwyn, who spent most of his time in the garden of the old priory at Hingham.

There is nothing in the section to suggest we are reading anything other than a piece of autobiographical prose, not even the sudden, though not entirely unexpected, suicide of Dr Selwyn, who shoots himself with a hunting rifle. The narrator comments: *When we received the news, I had no great difficulty overcoming the initial shock.*

But certain things, he goes on, *have a way of returning unexpectedly*. Some time after Dr Selwyn's death, the narrator, on a train in Switzerland, reads in a newspaper an account of the finding in the Swiss Alps of the preserved body of a Bernese alpine guide who disappeared in the summer of 1914; this man, Johannes Naegeli, was known to Dr Selwyn. Indeed, in the year before the beginning of the Great War, the two became so close that Selwyn said *never in his life, neither before nor later, did he feel as good as he did then, in the company of this man*. When Naegeli disappeared just after mobilisation began, Selwyn felt *it was as if I was buried under snow and ice*.

We are left in no doubt that the disappearance of Naegeli has always haunted Selwyn, and contributed to his long-premeditated suicide; nor can we question the veracity of the reported reappearance, 72 years later, of the alpine guide's body: in the book, poorly reproduced, but date-stamped and written in entirely convincing French, is a newspaper report of the event, photocopied from a Lausanne paper.

Or can we? We turn the page to section two of *The Emigrants* and find another suicide of another man in his twilight years, this time Sebald's former primary school teacher. You start to wonder. Is it possible that the newspaper account of the discovery of the body of the guide in the ice inspired the story about Selwyn's loss of love, and not the other way round? Was there perhaps a man of that name or another, known to Sebald, who took his life with a hunting rifle, yet never climbed in the Swiss Alps? Did he put together two or more unrelated events to form the vignette of Dr Henry Selwyn?

It is impossible to know. And therein lies the genius of Sebald's writing: he persuades you to read his work as autobiographical non-fiction then, with immense subtlety, manages to suggest that, on the contrary, it may be *made up*. And in that doubt about the status of what is before you, you read on with a preternatural attentiveness to detail.

W. G. Sebald is, in Pessoa's sense, an orthonym. As one writer put it:

Sebald's narrator is one W. G. Sebald, who lives
in Norfolk, comes from the German village of

W, and has a companion, Clara. Max Sebald was
born in Wertach im Allgäu in 1944 and lived in
an old rectory outside Norwich with his Austrian
wife, Ute, and their daughter, a school teacher.

Sebald was obsessively private and gave interviews
only rarely: *I don't want to talk about my trials
and tribulations. Once you reveal even part of what
your real problems might be in life, they come back in
a deformed way.* His sudden death, coming at a
time when he had reluctantly relinquished a larger
part of this privacy in order to publicise his last
book, *Austerlitz*, thus seems both perverse and
cruelly ironic.

Given the degree of artifice in his work, it is not
surprising that Sebald knew what he was doing:

> There was a vogue of documentary writing in
> Germany in the 1970s which opened my eyes.
> It's an important literary invention, but it's con-
> sidered an artless form. I was trying to write
> something saturated with material but carefully

wrought, where the art manifests itself in a discreet, not too pompous fashion ...

Every novelist combines fact and fiction. In my case, there's more reality. But I don't think it's radically different; you work with the same tools ... It's the opposite of suspending disbelief and being swept along by the action, which is perhaps not the highest form of mental activity; it's to constantly ask, "What happened to these people, what might they have felt like?" You can generate a similar state of mind in the reader by making them uncertain.

Elsewhere, he was sometimes scathing about the processes of the conventional novel, describing how, in the act of reading, you hear the machinery creak as the novelist constructs dialogue to advance the story, or moves characters around their artificial world to illustrate a theme. His own work is seamless, shifting time, place and voice the way these qualities shift in dreams.

There is something fluvial about Sebald's prose: to enter one of his works is to enter a river of language, which carries you along to confluences with other rivers, which also become part of the flow, until all of the tributaries meet and mingle in the great sea of silence which comes after the last page is turned.

His chosen voice is the first-person singular, but that voice is typically speaking of another individual who might then take up the narrative in his or her own voice, speaking of another, who might in their turn begin to speak: as if memory were not a solitary accomplishment, but requires contributions from us all.

The epigraph to that first short section of *The Emigrants* reads: *And the last remnants memory destroys.* All of Sebald's writing is about memory, but in what way? Sometimes it seems that he is saying, look, after all that has been swept away, these fragments remain; among all those who died, these people existed, these events happened.

On the other hand, as the epigraph implies, memory may itself be destructive. It has been suggested recently that memory does not record the events it seems to be about, but rather earlier memories of those events. Your childhood recall of the grassy track to the bull paddock, full of fear and urgent anticipation, is not a record of the actual journey you took down that path, but a palimpsest, the memory of a memory.

Memory is constructed out of fragments of past events, past people. However crucial it is for identity, it is still a *made up* record, not a true and verifiable one. We know this if we have ever tried to reconstruct an event – a car accident; the day Rachel died; that terrible argument – from multiple points of view. When Sebald says, *And the last remnants memory destroys*, is he saying that memory is also a fiction?

Sebald's four novels are book-ended by two works of non-fiction, both published posthumously – *After Nature*, his first literary composition, a long poem in three sections, and *The Natural History of Destruction*, a sustained meditation upon the place of memory in literature. *After Nature* is an evocative, indeed precognitive prelude to his works of fiction, while *The Natural History of Destruction,* which at a crucial point invokes Benjamin's Angel of History, can be read retroactively as commentary upon his own practice as a writer.

The title piece, a reworking of a series of lectures Sebald gave in Zurich in 1997, is an excoriating account of the Allied bombing campaign against German cities in the last three years of the Second World War, focused upon the almost complete suppression of discussion of these events not so much among the German people as among German writers. In the course of the essay Sebald introduces a concept, derived from Alexander Kluge, central to his own intentions as a writer: *retrospective learning*, defined as *the only way of deflecting human wishful thinking towards the anticipation of a future that would not already be pre-empted by the anxieties arising from the suppression of experience.* It is the literary equivalent of recovered memory syndrome.

The three essays that follow, on three writers (Alfred Andersch, Jean Améry and Peter Weiss) who were his contemporaries, likewise deal with the place of memory in their (very different) work. While the first is a polemic against Andersch's bad faith, the essays on the two latter writers analyse their attempts to write the unwriteable. They include passages which explore memory as affliction, as in those torture victims, like Améry himself, whose remembering as a function of identity is irredeemably scrambled, but whose recall of the actual torture they underwent is always with them. For such as these, memory is torment, and forgetting an unattainable grace.

This perhaps clarifies what Sebald's fictional chronicles are doing: they collapse the opposition of memory and forgetting, for that which is *made up* is neither remembered nor forgotten but exists in a different sense, a new thing added to the world.

Furthermore: *For those whose business is language, it is only in language that the unhappiness of exile can be overcome.*

If Sebald's main subject is memory, then the theatre of that memory is essentially Europe, and particularly, though not exclusively, Europe since the French Revolution. But this Europe of his, what is it? Does it exist? Or, should we say, more terribly, did it exist and is now destroyed?

Some recent histories – *Dark Continent: Europe's Twentieth Century* by Mark Mazower and *The Origins of Nazi Violence* by Enzo Traverso – suggest that the Nazi programme was not an aberration but a psychotic synthesis of various forms of violence refined in mainstream European civilisation during the nineteenth and early twentieth centuries: the mechanisation of capital punishment, the Panopticon, the production line, the growing popularity of biological metaphors in politics, racism, anti-Semitism, the imperial extermination of third and fourth world peoples. Sebald surely writes about *this* Europe, the Europe in which barbarism is a central, not a peripheral development. His is a generalised and non-partisan horror at what humanity has done, what we have become.

One way to read him, then, is as someone who tries to recover, with writing, what has been destroyed in the world. At the same time, in the melancholy fall of his sentences, and their preoccupation with loss, he suggests that such recovery is ultimately not possible. And yet he persisted, perhaps because writing was the only way he knew to link back to a lost past and thereby make another future possible.

The vehicle for the recovery of these losses is a free-floating intelligence called "W. G. Sebald", about whom we know almost nothing in an autobiographical sense. What we do know are his obsessions – architecture, graveyards, maps, photography, prisons, street names, zoos – and his emotions, which are precisely logged in all their overwhelming imprecision. And, as we read, it is indeed as if the Europe that has disappeared under the rubble of war is reconstituted as a simulacrum – not what was, so much as what might have been and therefore could yet be: a future in the past.

5

Baudelaire's de-haloed poet, Cavafy's hidden self, Pessoa's heteronyms, Benjamin's third person, Machado's Zero, Sebald's orthonym: who is the ghost who writes? As the author of three books and a few shorter works which are, in whole or in part, autobiographical narratives told in the first-person singular, shouldn't I have something to say about this?

But "I" is not me. It is as much a construction, and a strategy, as the other voices interrogated in this essay. Further, the process of the construction of this voice, I believe, does not differ in kind from other constructions, though the quality of the work it makes might. Perhaps a brief history is in order.

The Autobiography of My Father, which is a book of mourning, began out of frustration with poetry as a means of expression. I wanted to write about my father, yet when, on that beginning day, I went down the lane to the writing room I rented underneath a friend's kitchen in Darlinghurst, a feeling of intolerable weariness at the persona of my poetry came over me. I was sick of the sound of my own voice.

That was a liberating moment, and once I decided to try prose, in the first person, and address myself directly to my father, the writing flowed, without much anxious scanning back over what I'd written, nor any of those terrible moments of doubt which stop you mid-sentence at the wasteland or exitless maze you have got yourself into. The book, so unlike the troubled, ultimately clouded life of its alleged author, my father, had a charmed life.

Part of this ease came from that simple decision to address myself directly to him; part was because the longest section in the book is in fact a transcription of an actual conversation; part because there are other real documents embedded in the text, speaking for themselves. Perhaps for some readers there was a voyeuristic thrill to be had from the disclosure of this intimate material, though I know for others my father was and is a palpable presence between the covers.

My next book, *The Resurrection of Philip Clairmont*, could not have been more different. Instead of a few weeks, it took almost a decade to complete. Every possible difficulty, all of those the first book had flown blithely past, afflicted it. That long period in the 1990s during which I researched and wrote it remains in my mind an interminable haunting: sleepless nights, existential terrors, imaginary phantoms, actual apparitions.

Some of these problems reflected difficulties with subject matter; some were the consequence of my own uncertainty in the face of the task I had set myself: I was confronting real spectres both in the world and in myself. I'm reminded of the medium who felt she had to exorcise the Clairmont paintings she saw in the Govett-Brewster Art Gallery. I also remember the departure of the spirit of Philip Clairmont from me, a day during which I spent some time convulsing on a bed in the midst of what resembled a panic attack but which was, unlike a panic attack, followed by a feeling a great serenity. In this case the ghost who wrote was not entirely my own, but one I entertained for a time, along with the various other real or phantom presences it trailed.

There is a radical change of tone in that book, from the first-person autobiographical voice which narrates the first section to a neutral voice that tells the rest of the story. I was trying, in part two, to channel the artist, in part three, the art, with varying degrees of success. It's impossible to know now, but I sometimes wonder if, had I continued in the first person, I might have written a book which would have travelled into the larger world as a classic tale of an artist manqué.

That yearning to write a book straight through in one voice was the inception of *Chronicle of the Unsung*, which began as a phrase drifting unbidden into my head one day. This phrase, which I knew instantly was a title, carried with it no other information. I didn't know what it meant, nor did I know what the book was to be about. A lament for dead friends who'd never achieved their potential? A book about the obscure of the world? My own unsung exploits? In the end, I decided to take the title in a literal sense and apply it to parts of my own life story. In other words, to take some of the mass of my own failed, unfinished, unpublishable or just unpublished writings and see if I could string them together on an autobiographical thread. These included quite a few poems, a couple of diaries, the memory of the first 70-odd pages of a novel which I lost when I changed computers, two completed but unproduced screenplays, and miscellaneous other pieces, mostly ideas for essays which I'd noted down but never written up.

I was nervous about attempting autobiography: what possible justification could there be for that? Hence, every time I introduced myself, I jumped off as soon as possible into some other subject presumed to be of more interest or importance. This foregrounding of digression was an integral part of the conception of the book, but it wasn't an easy strategy to make work. Eventually I found I had to take myself seriously: the departures from autobiography wouldn't work unless I actually wrote autobiography. In this way, a book initially envisaged as quite impersonal has become in some respects exceedingly personal.

This was, however, an interesting process. One of the things I learned was that scepticism towards my own experience, while entirely justified, could nevertheless be turned to account. The way to unite disparate material in the same frame was through the use of a distinct voice. This voice would at once tell and doubt the story it told. It might also be described as a merger of the personal narration of part one of *The Resurrection of Philip Clairmont* with the neutral, channelling voice of the rest of the book; or as the naïve voice of *The Autobiography of My Father* grown up. Or even as a conversation between two voices, one personal, one laid open to other voices.

Part of the artifice of the personal voice is in its omissions: it is extremely partial autobiography. Each of the four sections of the book recounts a fragment of time, none longer than nine months, chosen essentially for its resistance to easy understanding. That is, they were difficult periods which were for that reason possible subjects for writing.

Another part of the construction of the voice is what is added: I suddenly found myself in a position where I no longer felt obliged, as I had previously, to present the documentary truth of my recollections. I felt free to include in the autobiographical narration inventions, exaggerations, possible truths. This was as liberating as not writing poems about my father. It doesn't matter what these inventions are: hopefully, it is the narrator's voice you come to trust, and if you do you will believe what it says; and in that belief the documentary truth or otherwise of the recollections becomes irrelevant. Those who doubt this might meditate upon the fact that the author of *Independence Day*, with its bitter-sweet evocation of a father-son relationship, has never had a child of his own.

Essentially the same point was made by Gabriel Garcia Marquez when he said in the recently published first volume of his autobiography what he learned from Kafka: *It was not necessary to demonstrate facts: it was enough for the author to have written something for it to be true, with no proofs other than the power of his talent and the authority of his voice.*

Despite the plethora of recent commentary about unreliable narrators, most readers still want to trust the inner revelations of character or thought an author presents them with. This need to believe what we read is deeply ingrained, so much so that even when we read the words of a known liar we still like to think we can distinguish truth from falsehood. In the same way, in our reading of non-fiction, we tend to believe, within certain constraints, those factual details about the world an author tells us.

In all cases, however, what we actually believe is the voice in which we are told these things, whether they be memories, inventions or so-called facts. If the voice is compelling enough, the status of the tale we're being told becomes extraneous, and this is just as true of factual writing as it is of imaginative writing.

Machado's Zero, like Mallarmé's blank page, is the beginning of all literary work. It is not so much a cancellation of what has gone before as an acknowledgement of it: the past like a great tsunami banks up behind us, sweeps over us, obliterating all we try to do as it rushes through the present to the make the future. To write at all is to reserve a space from this process of flux, to make a provisional clearing of the wreckage of history in which to build a structure which may alter the flow of time in some previously unthought way.

The self is a user illusion, thought the Dane, Tor Norretranders. And after all, the voice we carry in our heads is not unitary but threefold: the one who speaks our thought (our "self"), the one addressed (the "other"), and a third, the silent audience of both. This tripartite division is reiterated in reading, when the one who speaks (the author) is entertained by the one addressed (the reader), while the silent third listens. If and when this third loses interest, we put the book aside.

For some writers, the best way of accomplishing this dramatic transfer is through the use of a denatured voice, a stripped-down voice, an authorial voice that is not the author as personality but author as intent, with language its sole medium: *For those whose business is language, it is only in language that the unhappiness of exile can be overcome.* For others, it is the opposite. Only a voice which is not distanced from personal preoccupations can properly cross over from writer to reader. Writers like these may want to draw attention to their "I", not because it is infallible but because it is not.

I think of the Lucidity Institute, devoted to the theory and practice of Lucid Dreaming, or Dreaming True. We all know that fragments of reality enter into our dreams and are there transformed; but what if fragments of dreams enter into reality and transform it into something resembling a dream?

The exercise of the will over dreaming is one thing; the exercise of the dream's will is another. This is what authorship attempts. Writing, like lucid dreaming, is not so much a process of predicting a future as working out how to make one happen. And to do that you must first find a voice in which to tell it. If it is an authentic voice – one that can be believed – then what it says may well come true.

References

The following books were consulted and/or quoted from in this essay: *Poems of Fernando Pessoa*, ed. & trans. Edwin Honig and Susan Brown, Ecco Press, New York, 1986; *The Selected Prose of Fernando Pessoa*, ed. & trans. Richard Zenith, Grove Press, New York, 2001; *Collected Poems: C. P. Cavafy*, ed. George Savidis, trans. Edmund Keeley and Philip Sherrard, Chatto & Windus, London, 1979; *Illuminations: Walter Benjamin*, ed. with an introduction by Hannah Arendt, trans. Harry Zohn, Jonathan Cape, London, 1970; *Charles Baudelaire: A Lyric Poet in the Era of High Capitalism: Walter Benjamin*, trans. Harry Zohn, NLB, London, 1973; *For Walter Benjamin*, ed. Ingrid and Konrad Scheurmann, trans. Timothy Nevill; AsKI, Bonn, 1993; *The Arcades Project: Walter Benjamin*, trans. Howard Eiland and Kevin McLaughli, prepared on the basis of the German volume ed. Rolf Tiedemann; Belknap Press, Cambridge, Mass., 1999; *Times Alone: selected poems of Antonio Machado*, trans. Robert Bly, Wesleyan University Press, Middletown, Conn., 1983; *The Emigrants: W. G. Sebald*, trans. Michael Hulse, Harvill Press, London, 1997; *On the Natural History of Destruction: W. G. Sebald*, trans. Anthea Bell, Random House, New York, 2003.

Martin Edmond

ISBN 0-9582514-3-6